Without A Strategy:

The Strategy Planning Workbook

Bill Decker

Printed in the United States of America

ISBN 978-1-50853-052-7

Partners International, Inc.

Contents

Introduction to the Workbook: Without a Strategy

Without a strategy we are lost.

How do we even know if we've "won?" If we don't have a target and clear definable, measurable ways to hit our target, how can we determine our own success? In three decades I've had the chance to see firms try to build new products, enter new markets, acquire firms and reduce operational overhead all without a strategy. And I've seen many firms fail because of it.

As a management consultant, executives have asked me to build budgets without a strategy.

As an investor, I've heard pitches from firms who want funding. They've presented slide shows without a strategy.

This workbook is meant as a guide to help firms build a strategy. It won't tell a company what its goals and objectives are. The workbook provides a blueprint for firms to build their strategies, develop ways to measure them and help executives articulate those plans within and outside the organization.

Why do companies work without a strategy?

Simple. Executives are afraid that by planning a strategy, there will be more work. Nothing could be further from the truth. A strategy (or set of strategies) will refine and define activities. If activities aren't on the strategy, they should be avoided. It's a classic case of an overused phrase: work smarter not harder.

The Workbook is organized logically. It starts by helping the user understand the market, the firm itself and the directions being pursued. It asks the user to undergo common methodologies such as defining missions and visions. The user is then required to pull out actionable strategies, measurement techniques and list the parties responsible for fulfillment.

The Workbook has descriptions of what each section should contain and asks thought provoking questions. While this workbook is no substitute for trained facilitators and off site planning sessions, it should provide the strategic framework needed.

This workbook is best used in conjunction with an experienced, no nonsense facilitator. It is a guideline to use in strategic planning. Strategic planning should be done by a group of top executives or stakeholders in your business. A group of 3-6 people tends to work best. Dedicated executive time will build a strategy. Handing this workbook off to an underling and having it written up and emailed to the CEO will be a recipe for failure. My experience in 30 years has been that most firms will not spend the money or the time to prepare a proper, actionable strategic plan. For those of you who wish to "dabble" in strategy, this workbook will give you an outline.

Participants should be prepared, be ready with their homework and be willing to do homework afterwards to complete the strategic plan. Only by having full participation can a firm can insure that the strategy developed will actually be implemented.

Strategic planning sessions should be conducted off site, in 2-3 day sessions. My three rules are: no electronics such as cell phones, no outside calls and no grudges.

And when professional consulting and facilitation is needed, contact us at www.partnersinternational.com

Introduction Ideas Page

The Introductions Page(s) usually includes the following:

1. Welcome to the document/process

2. A word on the environment/dynamic changes occurring

3. Tie plan/document to any larger organizational/environmental context or vision

4. The purpose and rationale for the planning process – desired changes

5. A word on our vision (the vision explained)

6. The framework/strategic planning model that was used

7. Acknowledge/thanks to participants and key stakeholders involved in the Parallel Process

8. A word on implementation and our "core values" as key

9. A final challenge to all to support implementation

Strategic Plan for This Year: Introduction Sample

Welcome to Our Strategic Plan. This document is the dynamic blueprint for the growth of our firm through the end of next year. It is the product of intensive discussions by the Planning Committee members, feedback from regional meetings and correspondence with individual members. We have enlisted the services of Bill Decker of Partners International for Strategic Management as our planning consultant and facilitator. Bill has the rare ability to stimulate an intensive examination of his client's hopes and aspirations while adding his international perspective.

His guidance and encouragement throughout this process will contribute to the quality of this Strategic Plan as well as our implementation "Action Plan."

We now have a vision of where we want to be, an assessment of where we are now and a set of criteria to measure our progress. We have defined the values that describe how we do business and developed a list of strategics and priorities to move us from where we are to where we want to be.

The future is uncertain. We will always be faced with change, so we need to manage change rather than react to it. This planning process has provided us with a system to lead, manage, and change the Association in a well-planned, integrated manner based on our strategies. This systems approach also provides a management process that will change the way we do business day-to-day. The priorities from the plan become the priorities for our annual budgets, assuring that we focus our resources in those areas that move us toward our vision.

The Planning Committee is to be commended for their imagination, dedication, and perseverance throughout this process. The Core Planning Committee consisted of:

_____, _____,

_____, _____,

As the focus moved from strategies to specific actions, the committee was expanded to include the rest of the staff. A plan is of little value by itself. This document is the first step toward creating a high-performance, customer-focused organization that will benefit all stakeholders –our members, our employees, the board of directors and all those with whom we do business. I encourage each of you to take part in making our future happen.

Signed / Dated by:

CEO / Executive Director / Superintendent

Strategic Planning and Change Model

Topic Four Phases

Creating Our Ideal Future ....
A

Measurements of Success ....
B

Converting Strategies to Actions ....
C

Successful Implementation / Change ....
D

Environmental Scan Out to the Year and Beyond

Socio-Demographics / Employee Changes:

Competition / Industry and Substitutes Actions:

Economic Environment:

Political Climate:

Technology Projections:

Customer Changes:

Vision Details For the Upcoming Year; Objectives

Our vision statement describes ideally where and what we want to be in this year. These are the future hopes, dreams and aspirations for us. Are we the best of brand? The low cost supplier? The biggest, the best known, the most replaceable the most forward thinking? Who do we want to be?

Year Objectives

Year Objectives Details (Optional)

A

_____ :

Topic

_____ :

Topic

_____ :

Topic

_____ :

Topic

_____ :

Topic

_____ :

Mission Statement

Our mission statement outlines the purpose towards which we commit our work life. These are the reasons for the existence of our firm and it clearly describes who our customers are and what we produce as outcome benefits for them. This should be short and be able to be repurposed as a 30 second "elevator pitch."

Mission Details

Our Mission is:

Mission Details

A

(Optional)

B

C

Core Values

Our core values describe how we should act in order to accomplish the tasks leading to achieving our mission. They create our desired culture as they are the principles that guide the behaviors of all members of our firm. (i.e., Quality Service)

Core Value #1 Details

Core Value #2 Details

Core Value #3 Details

Core Value #4 Details

Key Success Factors (KSF)

Our key success factors arc our outcome measures of success. They measure how effectively our firm is achieving our vision, mission, and values on a year-by-year basis. It is our scoreboard for continuous improvement of success.

Measurement Areas* (in Priority) (Maximum of 10)

1. Leadership – Plan Achievement

2. Profitability of the Association

3. _____

4. _____

5. _____

6. _____

7. _____

8. _____

9. _____

10. _____

KSF First Year Action Plans

To fully develop your Key Success Factors matrix, fill out the following "To Do" list so KSFs are finalized. Often it takes most of the first year of implementation to finalize some KSFs and to get comfortable with their practical use. For this reason, we do not recommend getting final approval on KSF targets until then. In the final strategic planning document, include this action plan with KSF areas only. Below is a chart and each line item should contain the following 5 points:

Areas/Actions Needed/Target Measures/Who is Responsible/Date Due

1.

2.

3.

4.

5.

6.

7.

8.

9.

10.

Overall KSF Coordinator assigned to:

Organizational Goal Setting

Remember, goals are numbers. % increase in sales, % decrease in turnover, $ Sales, % market share, # staff, # clients, % returns

Key Success Factors

Who is Responsible to Measure This? Who is responsible to measure next year?

Baseline Data Goal

Area #1:

Factors:

Area #2:

Factors:

Area #3:

Factors:

Area #4:

Factors:

Area #5:

Factors:

Overall Coordinator is:

Current State Assessment: SWOTT

Most executives refer to this as a SWOT analysis (Strengths, Weaknesses, Opportunities and Threats). Add another T for Trends!

Strengths

(To build on)

Weaknesses

(To eliminate)

Opportunities

Threats

Trends

The 6 "Pieces" of Your Business; Porter Modeling

These 6 categories take a snapshot of your business. These factors are also the basis for a competitive analysis. Grade your firm along the continuum and grade your competitors next to you.

Inputs (raw materials. your product. your service)

_____

(F)   (A+)

Operations (how you do things)

_____

(F)   (A+)

Marketing (awareness, understanding and belief)

_____

(F)   (A+)

Sales (the juncture. yes or no)

_____

(F)   (A+)

Delivery (getting offerings to the clients)

_____

(F)   (A+)

Service (after the sale)

_____

(F)   (A+)

Marketplace Worksheet

Instructions:

Define A through F below for this year or the next two or three years

Top 3 Market Segments

Characteristics

1.

2.

3.

A. Key Customers

B. Main Products and Services

C. Value of Market Segment (H-M-L)

———————————————————

D. Market Share

——————————

E. Competitors

————————

Inputs/operations/marketing/sales/delivery/service

F. Industry's Life Cycle

———————————————

Core Strategies (Samples)

Our core strategies are the primary means and methods we will use to move our firm from today to our firm's vision for the next year.

Core Strategies are the primary ways we "close the gap" between today and our firm desired Future Objectives. Thus, they are also the "glue" and "organizing framework" for all parts of the organization. They replace the obsolete concept of separate department goals. These are core strategies for each department.

1. Financial and Leadership Stability (Title)

Improve our firm long-term financial and leadership stability through continual

implementation of the Strategic Plan. (Strategy Statement)

2. Existing Programs and Services

Improve existing programs, customer service, communication and interactions

among staff and members.

3. New Programs and Services

Develop and implement new programs and services that will enhance the

value of our product.

4. Marketing

Assist the marketing both by providing specific marketing services and by improving the industry awareness and acceptance of our suite of offerings

5. Education (Training) Program

Implement an education program to increase the skills and industry knowledge of our staff and members.

6. Alliances

Pursue and develop alliances with other companies, international registries, and

industry segments.

7. Competitive analysis (ongoing)

8. New Business Development

9. Customer Retention

10. Talent Acquisition

Strategic Actions for Each Strategy

Core Strategy #1 (Title)

To: (Strategy Statement)

How is it changing? Actions:

From: 1.

2.

To:

3.

4.

(Short, clear phrases only)

5.

6.

7.

8.

9.

10.

11.

12.

13.

14.

15.

Core Strategy #2
_____

To: Sales plan. (1 for each customer)

How is it changing? Actions:

From: 1.

2.

To:

3.

4.

(Short, clear phrases only)

5.

6.

7.

8.

9.

10.

Without a Strategy

11.

12.

13.

14.

15.

38

Major Change Summary

A summary of the major changes desired over the entire life of our Strategic Plan.

1.

2.

3.

4.

5.

6.

7.

8.

9.

10.

11.

12.

13.

14.

15.

16.

17.

18.

Annual Top Priority Actions

These are the key "Must Do" actions – focus, focus, and focus – in addition to both (1) the day-to-day operations, and (2) any other tasks you can complete in addition to these "Must Do's."

	Core Lead	Top Strategies	Accountability

1. (Title)

_____1.

_____2.

_____3.

2. (Title)

_____1.

_____2.

_____3.

3. (Title)

_____1.

_____2.

_____3.

4. (Title)

_____1.

_____2.

_____3.

Implementation Game Plan

General Points on Change:

Our key implementation process will include these main items:

1. Strategic Change Steering Committee. This group will monitor implementation of the strategies, achievement of Key Success Factor targets, and the external environment for issues that could affect our plans and require changes to them.

2. Strategy Sponsorship / Project Teams are composed of members with a strong interest in a particular core strategy. These teams will lead and monitor the progress of each strategy and recommend actions needed to achieve that strategy.

3. Annual Department Plans will be developed by all Department Heads and reviewed/critiqued by our collection leadership each year.

4. Strategic Review / Update. Each (Pick time period) we will update our Plan (i.e., Annual Strategic Review and Update) to keep the priorities current.

5. Leadership Development Board

6. Technology Steering Group

7. Weekly Executive Staff Meetings

8.

Primary Change Management

Sample Structures and Roles

1. Visionary Leadership – CEO / Senior Executives with Personal Leadership Plans (PLPs)

- For repetitive stump speeches and reinforcers
- To ensure fit / integration of all parts and people towards the same vision

2. Internal Support Cadre (informal / kitchen cabinet)

- For day-to-day coordination of implementation process
- To ensure the change structures and processes don't lose out to day-to-day

3. Executive Committee

- For weekly meetings and attention
- To ensure follow-up on the top 15-25 priority yearly actions

4. Strategic Change Leadership Steering Committee (formal)

- For bimonthly / quarterly follow-up meetings to track and adjust
- To ensure follow-through via a yearly comprehensive map of implementation

5. Strategy Sponsorship Teams

- For each core strategy
- To ensure achievement of each one

6. Employee Development Board

- For succession, careers, development, core competencies (all levels) performance management / appraisals
- To ensure fit with our desired values / culture and employees as a competitive edge

7. Technology Steering Committee

- For computer and telecommunications software fit and integration
- To ensure "system-wide" fit / coordination around information management

8. Communications System and Structure

- For clear two-way dialogue and understanding of the Plan / implementation
- To ensure everyone is heading in the same direction with the same strategies

9. Measurement and Benchmarking Team

- For collecting and reporting of Key Success Factors
- To ensure an outcome / customer focus at all times

10. Annual Department Plans

- For clear and focused department plans that are critiqued, shared and reviewed

- To ensure a fit, coordination and commitment to the core strategies top priorities

11. Parallel Process

- For input and involvement of all key stakeholders before a decision affecting them is made

- To ensure a critical mass in support of the vision and desired changes

Strategic Change Road Map

Date Meetings

Month 1

Month 2

Month 3

Month 4

Month 5

Month 6

Month 9

Month 12

Month 24

Month 36

Comprehensive Year Implementation Map

Date Meetings

1.   Month 1 Begin Strategic Planning (Plan-to-Plan: 2 day)

2. Month 2 Do Strategic Planning (5-8 days overall)

3. Month 2 Develop Annual Work Plans/Budgets

4. Month 3 Conduct Large Group Department Plan Review (1 day)

5. Month 3 Conduct Plan-to-Implement (1 day)

6. Month 6 Quarterly Steering Committee Review Session (or bimonthly)

7. Month 9 Quarterly Steering Committee Review Session (or bimonthly)

8. Month 12 Evaluate Plan's Year #1 Success (rewards based on this)

9. Month 24 Conduct Annual Strategic Review (and Update: 2-4 days overall)

10. Month 36 Develop 3-Year Business Plans (for Business Units)

11. Month 48 Develop Updated Annual Department Work Plans/Budgets

12. Month 48 Conduct Large Group Department Plan Review (1 day)

13. Month 51 Quarterly Steering Committee Review Session (or bimonthly)

14. Month 54 Quarterly Steering Committee Review Session (or bimonthly)

15. Month 60 Institutionalized— Strategic Review/Update Again (as a way of life)

Shopping List

This is what is missing! Write down what needs to be gathered, researched, bought or understood. Who will acquire the items on the shopping list and when?

Summary

This should be a 1-page summary of the strategy. This should be written in terms simple enough for my mother (or anyone's mother) to understand it. After writing it, take the one page conclusion to someone who knows very little about your business and see if he or she understands it.

Conclusion to Workbook

So are we with or without a strategy? If a strategy has been properly prepared, it should be easy to read articulate and summarize. It should have realistic goals and objectives that make sense. There should be a list of what needs to be changed and how that will happen. And there should be a timetable that is adhered to. The process could be exhausting, so try to make it fun!

For additional help and useful links, try:

http://partnersinternational.com

Many useful articles and tools

http://lemonaderadio.com

Online radio show about strategy and business, sweetened with humor

http://internationaltoolkit.com

Podcast on international business

http://internationalbusinessminute.com

International business videos

http://lessonsfromtheroad.com

A blog of free business articles

http://marketentrytoolkit.com

A toolkit showing how to choose and enter a foreign market

I hope this workbook will help you proceed with a strategy.

Email me:

info@partnersinternational.com

www.ingramcontent.com/pod-product-compliance
Lightning Source LLC
Chambersburg PA
CBHW080607180526
45168CB00007B/2811

* 9 7 8 1 5 0 8 5 3 0 5 2 7 *